THE GREAT EVIL

REVEREND JOHN FURNISS, C.S.S.R.

CATHOLIC WAY
PUBLISHING

Copyright © 2013 by Catholic Way Publishing.
All rights reserved.

Copyright © 1900 by Duffy, Dublin, Ireland.
Retypeset and republished in 2013 by Catholic Way Publishing.
Cover design by Catholic Way Publishing.

APPROBATION

"I have carefully read over this Little Volume for Children and have found nothing whatsoever in it contrary to the doctrine of Holy Faith; but, on the contrary, a great deal to charm, instruct and edify our youthful classes, for whose benefit it has been written."

William Meagher, Vicar General, Dublin, December 14, 1855.

5" x 8" Paperback. Also available as an E-Book.
Kindle: ISBN-13: 978-1-78379-239-9
EPUB: ISBN-13: 978-1-78379-240-5

This work is published for the greater Glory of Jesus Christ through His most Holy Mother Mary and for the sanctification of the militant Church and her members.

The typography of this book is the property of Catholic Way Publishing and may not be reproduced, in whole or in part, without written permission of the Publisher.

10 9 8 7 6 5 4 3 2 1

ISBN-13: 978-1-78379-238-2

ISBN-10: 1-78379-238-8

CATHOLIC WAY
PUBLISHING

WWW.CATHOLICWAYPUBLISHING.COM
LONDON, UK
2013

CONTENTS

※

CHAPTER I.
WHAT IS THE GREAT EVIL?...............1

CHAPTER II.
WHY IS MORTAL SIN THE GREAT EVIL?...............2

CHAPTER III.
THE HARDNESS OF MORTAL SIN...............3

CHAPTER IV.
THE SENTENCE AGAINST MORTAL SIN...............4

CHAPTER V.
HOW HE DIES WHO COMMITS A MORTAL SIN...............7

CHAPTER VI.
THE FRIGHTFULNESS OF A SOUL IN MORTAL SIN...............12

CHAPTER VII.
LOSS...............16

CHAPTER VIII.
THE DEVILS...............26

CHAPTER IX.
MORTAL SIN WRITTEN IN CHARACTERS OF FIRE...............31

CHAPTER X.
THE VOICE OF GOD TO THE SINNER...............32

CHAPTER XI.
MORTAL SIN WRITTEN IN CHARACTERS OF BLOOD...............34

CHAPTER XII.
THE VOICE OF JESUS ON THE CROSS TO THE SINNER...............36

CHAPTER XIII.
THE VOICE OF THE SINNER TO JESUS...............37

CHAPTER XIV.
THE FUTURE...............38

CHAPTER I

WHAT IS THE GREAT EVIL?

SOME children were learning their Catechism; the teacher asked them this question: "What is the worst thing in the world?" A little child put up its hand and said, Please, may I answer? Yes, said the teacher. Then, said the child, I think the worst thing in the world is a great pain. The child did not give the right answer. No doubt it is frightful to see any one burnt up with fever, or cramped with cholera, or to see death tearing away the soul from the body. It is a sad thing to say the last "good bye" to those whom we love. These things make tears run down from the eye and draw sighs out of the heart. But there is something which burns more than fever, and cramps more than cholera. There is a last parting more sorrowful than the last parting with father, mother, brother, or sister.

What, then, is the great bad thing? The greatest of all evils—the evil of evils—what is it? The greatest of all evils is—Mortal sin. Mortal sin is so great an evil that no man living will be able to understand how great an evil it is. *Ps. xviii.* "Who shall understand sins?"

CHAPTER II

WHY IS MORTAL SIN THE GREAT EVIL?

"To thee only have I sinned." Ps. i.

"Thou hast broken my yoke and burst my bonds, thou hast said, I will not serve." Jer. ii. A child was bid by its father to go on an errand; the child answered, "I shan't go, I won't go." Everybody who heard this answer was shocked. How shocking, then, must it be when any one says to Almighty God, the God who has in his hands thy breath and all thy ways, who can cast a body and soul into hell, "Oh, God! I shall not, I will not do what you bid me!" *Mal. iii.:* "Shall a man afflict God?" It is Sunday, and you know well that God commands you to hear Mass. You could go to Mass if you liked, there is nothing to hinder you. You refuse to go to Mass; you stop away by your own fault, and commit a mortal sin. It is as if you spoke thus to God: "O Almighty God! I know that you are my Creator, and I am your creature; I know that I ought to obey you and keep your commandments; I know that if I break your commandments, I deserve to go to hell for it. And now I tell you, O God, that I will not keep your commandments. You command me to go to Mass to-day, and I tell you that I will not go to Mass; I will not do your will, but my own will; I know that I deserve to go to hell for it, but I do not care for that." Wicked child! "you know not what you do," when you thus break the commandments of God; *Luc. xxiii. 34.* God wonders that his own creatures, whose body and soul he can cast into hell, should dare thus to despise him. Thus he speaks, *Is. i.:* "Hear, O ye heavens, and give ear, O earth, for my people have despised me." He must have a hardened heart who dares thus to despise the majesty of God.

CHAPTER III

THE HARDNESS OF MORTAL SIN

※

A ROCK is hard, but a drop of water always falling upon a rock will wear it away. Iron is hard, but fire will burn it away. One only thing there is which no fire, not even the fire of hell, can burn away—and that one thing is mortal sin. See first the difference betwist the fire of Earth and the fire of Hell. Take a spark out of the kitchen fire, drop it in a river, and it will go out directly. But the fire of hell is "kindled in God's wrath." *Deut. xxxii.* Take, then, one very little spark out of the fire of hell, less in size than a pin's head—cast that spark of hell into the waters of the ocean. Would it go out? No, it would blaze out in the waters, and set them on fire, and in one moment the whole earth would be in a blaze and burnt to ashes. The fire of hell then is strong, but there is something stronger than the fire of hell, and that is mortal sin. Put a mortal sin into the very midst of the raging flames of hell. These flames burn above and below and on every side, and in the midst of mortal sin. Do these fierce flames burn it away? No; when the mortal sin shall have been in the midst of the burning flames for millions and millions of years, it will be just as hard, heavy, and black as it was at the beginning. What does this mean? I will tell you. A man dies, and there is in his dying heart the malice and the wilful intention of not going to Mass on Sunday, or of doing some immodest action. He is dead, and condemned to hell. In hell this evil intention remains in his heart just as on earth, and he would not give it up even to get out of the flames of hell. There is no repentance in hell. O sinner, there is a just and terrible God, who repays sin forthwith, with the blast of the spirit of his wrath; *Ps. xvii. 7.*

CHAPTER IV

THE SENTENCE AGAINST MORTAL SIN

GOD said to Adam, "In whatsoever day thou shalt eat of the tree of knowledge of good and evil, thou shalt die the death." *Gen. ii*. To every creature the same words are said. In whatever day thou shalt break the commandments of God, thou shalt die. Therefore, if on Sunday, you stop from Mass by your own fault, or if you do some immodest thing, there is the sentence: "Thou shalt die the death." *Dan. v.* : Baltassar was king of Babylon. Babylon was a great city, 60 miles round; the streets were 15 miles long; the king's palace 7 miles round. Baltasaar made a feast for a thousand of his nobles. They sang songs, and drank wine till they were drunk. Drunkenness brings with it many other sins. When the king was drunk he said, Bring in the vessels which have been used in the service of God, and we will drink out of them. It was a sacrilege to show this disrespect to vessels used in God's service. Then at the king's command the holy vessels were brought in, and the king and his nobles drank out of them. They sang hymns to their false gods made of metal and stone. In the midst of their songs suddenly there was a dead silence—what was the matter? the king had looked up, and he had seen the fingers, as it were, of a hand at the wall over against the great candlestick. Those fingers were writing letters on the wall, but they were letters such as no eye had ever seen before. Then the face of the king was changed with fear. He turned pale, and his knees struck one against the other. He cried out for the wise men to come, that they might tell him the meaning of those words which had been written. The wise men came, but when they had seen the letters, they said they could neither read the letters nor tell the meaning of them. And now it came to the ears of the queen, how fingers, as it were, of a hand, had been writing on the wall letters which nobody could read. The queen came in haste, and stood before the king, and spoke to him thus: "O king," she said, "do not be troubled. There is in your kingdom one whose name is Daniel, a prophet of the true God. In the days of your father, knowledge and wisdom were found in him. Let him be sent for." The prophet Daniel was sent for. "O Daniel," said the king to him, "I have heard that you have the spirit of wisdom and knowledge, that you can tell the meaning of hidden things. Now, then, if you are able to read that writing, and tell the meaning of it, you shall be clothed in purple, and have a chain of gold about your neck, and you shall be the third prince in my kingdom." Then Daniel answered the king and said: "O king, keep your rewards for others, but the writing I will read, and tell you the meaning of it. O king, the most high God gave to Nabuchodnosor, your father, a kingdom, and greatness, and honor, and glory. All people, and tribes, and languages trembled before him. His heart was lifted up, and his spirit was hardened with pride. Then he was put down from the throne of his kingdom, and his glory was taken way. He was driven out from the sons of men, and his heart was made like the heart of beasts, and his dwelling was with wild asses, and he did eat grass like an ox. His body was wet with the dew of heaven, till he knew that the Most High rules in the kingdom of men, and sets over it whomsoever it shall please him. Thou also, his son, O King Baltassar, hast not humbled thy heart. When thou knewest all these things, thou hast lifted up thyself against the God of Heaven. The holy vessels have been brought in before thee, and thou and thy nobles have drunk out of them. Thou hast praised the gods made of gold, and silver, and of stone, and wood, which neither see, nor hear, nor feel. But the God who has in his hands thy breath and all thy ways thou hast not glorified. Therefore, God has sent that hand to write what is written. This, then, is the writing: Mane, Thekel, Phares. And this is the meaning of the words: Mane—God hath numbered thy kingdom. Thekel—thou art weighed in the balance and found wanting. Phares—Thy kingdom is divided and given to the Medes and Persians." Then, by the king's command, Daniel was clothed in purple, and a chain of gold was put about his neck, and it was proclaimed that he had power as the third man in the kingdom. The same night King Baltassar was killed, and the Medes and Persians took possession of his kingdom.

Little child, when you commit a mortal sin, you also lift yourselves up against the God of Heaven, for you refuse to obey him; you sacrilegiously profane your soul, which is the holy and precious vessel of God, and his dwelling place, and you give glory to the devil, who is the enemy of God. In that moment, when you thus commit a mortal sin, there is a hand writing dark letters, the letters of death, on your soul; and this is the writing: *Thou shalt die the death.* The handwriting is written on your understanding, for you know you are dead before God; it is written on your memory, and the remembrance of the death sentence will haunt your memory; it is written on your will, because of your own free will you have chosen death rather than life. Nobody on earth can see those words of death which are written on your soul, neither your father, your mother, or brothers, or sisters. But God sees them, and the angels see them. But what is the meaning of those fearful words, *Thou shalt die the death?* The meaning of them you shall know, for God has said, "As I have spoken, so will I do to the wicked." *Numbers xiv.*

CHAPTER V

HOW HE DIES WHO COMMITS A MORTAL SIN

※

1. *Thou shalt die the death. Gen. ii.* You have committed a mortal sin. Then, you are dead; "for the wages of sin is death." *Rom. vi.* Yes, O sinner, you are dead! But how can you be dead? Your face is not pale as the face of the dead; you are not cast down on the earth a corpse; no coffin is brought to you, no grave is dug for you. Who would say that you are dead? You breathe, you eat, you talk, you laugh, just as you did before the hour when the mortal sin was committed. Can it be true, then, that you are dead? Yes, O sinner, it is most true that you are dead. As sure as the God of Heaven has said, "Thou shalt die the death," so surely are you dead, and "you belong to him who has the empire of death, that is, the devil." *Heb. ii.*

What, then, is that death which has stricken you? "Your body is not slain by the sword, nor dead in battle." *Is. xxii.* Listen, then, O sinner, and I will tell you how death has stricken you. "The soul that sinneth," says the prophet, "the same shall die." *Ezech. xviii.* The mortal sin which you committed, quick as a flash of lightning struck your soul dead. *Is. xxix.* "It shall be in an instant, suddenly."

But how does all this happen? Listen: It is the moment of temptation; the soul is tempted to break the commandments of God, and commit a mortal sin. Oh, the terrible moment for the soul. *Ps. xvii.:* "The sorrows of death surround it." There is silence in heaven; the angels speak not; God is looking at the soul to see what will it do. Will it consent to the temptation or not? All is over; the soul has consented to the temptation, and committed the mortal sin. Oh, the crash, the breaking, the ruin!

Is it an earthquake which has torn the earth in pieces, or the sun darkened, or the moon turned red as blood, or the stars falling from heaven? No; none of these things. It is something more frightful. A thunderbolt from hell has broken in pieces God's greatest work—a soul is ruined. O God, that immortal soul, which was created in your image and likeness, and redeemed with the blood of Jesus Christ, is crushed and ruined! The wailings of the angels are not heard from heaven, neither do the blasphemies of the devils in hell come to the ear. All has been done in silence, and that soul is lying a silent ruin on the face of God's earth. O sinner, after the mortal sin you go into your house, and the stone does not cry out from the wall against your dead soul; you pass through the country, and the beasts in the field do not roar out because a dead soul is passing in the midst of them; you go along the street, and the people you meet do not run away from your dead soul. But there is One who sees your dead soul. There is a God in heaven who sees your dead soul, and hates the sight of it. *Wisd. xiv.* "The wicked and his wickedness are alike hateful to God."

Oh, the day of mortal sin! Oh, that day, that terrible day, when a soul died which had once breathed the breath of life! Oh, the day of mortal sin; "the day of death;" that day is a day of wrath, a day of tribulation and distress, a day of calamity and misery; *Soph. ii.* "Let that day be turned into darkness; let not God regard it from above; let not the light shine upon it; let the darkness and shadow of death cover it." *Job. ii.*

2. *They shall mourn over him. Ezech. xxvii.* A boy dies. His little sister goes to her mother, and says: Please, mother, may I put on mourning for my brother who is dead? The mother answers, Yes, my child, you shall put on mourning for your poor brother. The black clothes come; and the child is dressed in a black frock, black bonnet, black shawl, black gloves. Thus the body, which was not created to the image and likeness of God, dies, and for a dead body there is mourning. Nay, even a senseless beast sinks down in the fields and dies, and for a dead beast there is sorrow; but a soul created to the image and likeness of God dies by mortal sin, and for a dead soul no cry is heard, no tear is shed. He who once was just perisheth, and no man layeth it to heart,

Is. lvii.; as if God had not said: "They shall mourn over him and be girded with sackcloth." *Ezech. xxviii.*

3. *They shall cry bitterly over thee. Ezech. xvii.* Some years have now passed since a missioner was giving a mission to the children in one of those small squares in London called courts. It was winter time. The children received an instruction in the morning, and again in the evening, and made their confessions. One evening the instruction went on as usual. Suddenly there was an interruption, the missioner stopped in the midst of his instruction; what was the matter? A noise was heard at the door, and in a few minutes the door was burst open with violence; a woman rushed in, and walking with haste through the midst of the children, she came up to the platform where the missioner was, and there she stood for a moment, speechless and breathless. What is the matter, my good woman? said the missioner. Oh, father, she said, make haste and come quick, my husband has fallen on the floor, and he is dying! The missioner followed the woman in haste. Going up a narrow staircase, he entered the room where the dying man was. The poor man lay on the floor; large drops of sweat ran down his pale face; his eyes were rolling in their sockets, his breathing short and difficult, and the death-rattle in his throat. It was a fearful sight to see the man in the agony of death, while his soul was passing out of this world to the judgement-seat of God. But there was another sight still more sorrowful. Around the dying father knelt his five little children, and well they knew what the matter was—they knew that their poor father was dying. Oh! the sorrow, the grief of those poor children! They were crying, and wailing, and sobbing over their poor father in the agony of death. Little child, it may be that death has been in your house as well as in the house of which I speak. Perhaps in your house it was a more frightful death—the death of the soul by mortal sin. How was it that death came into your house? Perhaps it was Sunday, and your brother lost Mass by his own fault; then he came home to you with a dead soul in him, killed by mortal sin. When, then, he opened the door, and brought a dead soul into the midst of you, did you all, brothers and sisters, come round and cry, and sob, and wail, and scream for his poor dead soul? Did you say: O brother, your poor soul is dead? Poor soul! we cry for you broth-

er, and the tears run down from our eyes because your soul is dead? *Ezech. xxvii.:* "They shall mourn over thee with a loud voice and cry bitterly; they shall weep for thee with bitterness of soul, and with most bitter weeping."

4. *They died for fear. Wis. xvii.* O sinner, it may be that your eye sees something that brings death to your remembrance. It is, perhaps, the waving plume of a dark hearse which is carrying a dead body to its last home, or perhaps it is the pale face of a corpse. Then fear strikes your heart; for the remembrance of thee, O death, is bitter; *Eccus. xli.* O sinner, you carry death within you—you have a dead soul within you, and you are not afraid. There was a little child which had never seen a dead body in its life. It happened that some one died in the house where the child was living. In the evening the child was taken up-stairs to the room where the dead body was laid on a bed. By the pale light of a candle this child, for the first time in its life, saw a dead body! The poor child trembled when it saw the strange paleness of the dead face—the eyes fixed, the lips which breathed no more, the hands which moved not, and the wonderful stillness and quiet of that dead body. The people said to the child: You shall stop here all night, in the dark, without any light, alone by yourself with the dead body. Then they all went out, leaving the child alone with the dead body. They remained standing outside, wishing to see if the child would be frightened. A few moments passed and they heard a frightful scream, and immediately afterwards the sound, as it were, of something falling heavily on the floor. They opened the door, and saw that the child was lying on the floor. They went to lift it up, and found that it was dead! the fright of being left alone in the dark with the dead body had killed the poor child. O sinner, in the darkness of the night you are alone, not with a dead body, but with a dead soul! and you are not afraid; but if God opened your eyes to see that frightful, hideous monster of a dead soul which is in you, you would never rise again from your bed. The sight of that fearful, terrible dead soul in you, would take away your breath, and your sense, and your life.

5. *There shall be a reproach among the dead forever. Wis. iv.* The fifth commandment says: "Thou shalt not kill." By the old law of England, the dead body of any man who had murdered himself

was laid on a board. In the dead of the night the body was taken out of the house lying on the board. Then it was borne away out of the town, and carried along the lonesome country roads, till it was brought to a place where there were four cross-roads. The dead body was set down there. By the light of a lantern they dug a deep hole with pickaxes and spades. Then the dead body was lifted up and thrown down to the bottom of this hole. Then the hole was filled up again; and so he who murdered himself was buried as a dog is buried. Then the people said: Here are four roads crossing one another, and many people pass this way; let, then, every foot trample on the grave of the man who murdered himself. Wicked sinner, self-murderer! when you committed that mortal sin, you did not murder your mortal body, but you murdered your own immortal soul, into which God had breathed the breath of life; and you sought to have been buried with the burial of a dog. *Jer. xxii.* "He shall be buried with the burial of an ass, rotten and cast forth." Oh, soul! murdered, slain, receiving the death wound from your own hand—how ghastly, how frightful you are!

CHAPTER VI

THE FRIGHTFULNESS OF A SOUL IN MORTAL SIN

1. For what shall I strike you any more? The whole head is sick, the whole heart is sad. From the sole of the foot to the top of the head there is no soundness therein, but wounds and bruises, and swelling ulcers. Is. i. If you look into a looking-glass you see your face in it. Poor child in mortal sin, let me put before you a looking-glass, that you may see a little the frightfulness of your soul. There is a miserable body—all its bones are broken in pieces—the skull is broken, the back-bone broken, the arms broken, the legs broken, the bones in the hands and feet broken, all the flesh and skin is torn in pieces and stripes. Every disease in the world is in that body; there is typus fever, yellow-fever, scarlet-fever, cholera, and plague. There is consumption in the lungs, jaundice in the liver, disease in the heart, blindness in the eyes, deafness in the ears, toothache, and every pain that comes upon men. O sinner, your soul is a million times worse. When you committed that mortal sin, "the vial of God's wrath was poured upon you, and a sore and grievous wound fell upon your soul." Apoc. xvi. O soul, O soul in mortal sin, stricken with that sore and grievous wound—a death's wound. Apoc. xiii. Whence came that wound, that incurable wound in your soul? Did it, like the sickness of the body, come by some accident; from a little damp, or from a change in the air? No; that wound in your soul came not from any change in the air, but from a change of the Almighty Spirit to you. He who once was your Father, has poured out the vial of his anger and indignation oon your soul, and stricken it with a sore and grievous wound; and the stroke

which made that wound in your soul, was such as the hand of Almighty God, in his anger, alone could strike.

2. *Sepulchres, full of dead men's bones and all filthiness. Mat. xxiii.* In the neighborhood of a certain town there is a large burial-ground, in which there are three hundred and sixty-five large vaults or graves, each of them large enough to hold hundreds of dead bodies; these graves are not filled up with earth, but over the top is placed a large, heavy, square stone; each day of the year one of these vaults is opened, and all the dead who have to be buried on that day are buried in the one vault. It is the custom for the dead bodies to be thrown in the vault without any coffin. It happened that one day a person went and lifted the large stone which covered one of these vaults. Oh, what a sight! there you might see death. There were hundreds of dead bodies; some lay on the ground with their faces looking upwards, others with their faces turned to the earth; some of the dead bodies were leaning against the wall, some with their white skeleton hands stretched out as if pointing; there were eyes dropping out of their sockets, ears falling off, teeth away from the jaw, hair scattered on the ground; arms and feet separated from their bodies; bones piercing through the skin. This immense mass of livid and rotting flesh was of every color from pale to black. In some the flesh was hard; in others, dissolved like water. There were thousands and thousands of reptiles feeding on the dead flesh. The smell of the corrupting flesh of these bodies was insufferable, so that if he who lifted up the stone had not quickly put it down again, he would have fallen down dead into the midst of the dead bodies in the vault. O sinner, give ear to the words of Jesus Christ, for he calls you "a sepulchre, full of dead men's bones and all filthiness." *Mat. xxiii.* O soul in mortal sin! you are, then, like a deep grave filled with corruption; not the corruption of flesh, or of blood, but with the corruption of spirit, corruption of thoughts and desires, of words and actions. Now, if the corruption of the body is bad, the corruption of the soul must be a great deal worse, because the better a thing is, the worse its corruption is. O soul in mortal sin! you are a grave filled with diabolic corruption, with infernal corruption; still you are a grave closed up, a sealed monument; no eye can look in. On the outside it may appear that you are beautiful with satins and silks, with orna-

ments of gold and silver. But there will come a day when the sound of the last trumpet will break the seal and burst open the grave, then every eye shall see your soul as it is—the most horrible, frightful, abominable sight that can be. *Is. lxvi.* "They shall go out and see the carcases of the men that have sinned against me, a loathsome sight to all flesh."

3. *For my iniquities are gone over my head, and as a heavy burden are become heavy upon me. Ps. xxxvii.* O sinner, when you carry about with you a soul dead in mortal sin, do you know what a terrible and frightful load you are carrying? There was a certain man condemned to suffer an extraordinary punishment. It happened long since; it was in the times of the Pagans, before the Christian religion was on earth. There was a dead body, black, as if it had died of the black cholera. This black body was fastened to the body of the criminal, and it was so fastened that it was impossible for him to get free from it. The wretched man trembled and shook with terror when he saw the terrible load coming which he was to carry. When he felt the weight of it pressing upon him, the feeling of death pierced his very bones. This was only the beginning of his misery. The dreadful load was always pressing upon him; in the light of the day he saw with his eyes the frightful load of black death which he carried, in the darkness of night the dead body was his only companion; the smell of that horrible dead body was most fearful. From the corruption of death worms began to come, and they crept into his mouth, and eyes, and ears, and nostrils. Never was there such an awful sight. The people who saw this man at a distance shrieked with fright and ran away; the very beasts fled away when he passed. The unfortunate man himself howled with terror and pain; he bit his tongue, and dashed himself against the stones. At length he lost his senses, and fell down dead under the terrible load which he carried. Unhappy sinner! you go about, day by day, bound up with death—not the black cholera death, or the death of flesh and blood—but the real death, the death of the spirit, that death which came out of hell. Poor sinner! shall you then be left to perish under this crushing load? Must you go about howling with fright, biting your tongue in despair, and dashing yourself against stones, losing your senses, and at last falling down into the flames of hell? Is your wound incurable? *Jer. viii.* "Is there no

balm in Gilead, is there no physician?" Poor sinner? think not so. You shall, if you wish it, be delivered from this body of death. But who shall deliver you? The grace of God by Jesus Christ our Lord. *Rom. viii.*

But you have not heard the worst of mortal sin—the worst is yet to come. *Is. vi.* "God's anger is not yet turned away, his hand is stretched out still."

CHAPTER VII

LOSS

※ ※

1. THE LOSS OF GOD, OR THE ABOMINATION OF DESOLATION.—*The Lord has departed from thee! Kings xxviii.* Poor sinner, you do not yet know what is that most terrible thing in the death of the soul! If you were ever in a death chamber just the moment after the soul has left the body, you would notice what a wonderful frightful lonesomeness there is about the body, how desolate it looks when the soul has just left it. O sinner, if the body be lonesome when the soul has departed from it, how lonesome must the soul be, when God its Creator has left it in the moment of mortal sin? The death of the body is the soul going away from it, but the death of the soul is when God leaves and abandons the soul on account of mortal sin—for "the breath of our mouth Christ the Lord is taken away in our sin," *Lam. iv.;* and "the Holy Spirit will not abide when iniquity cometh in." *Wisd. i.* Know then, O sinner, and see that it is an evil and a bitter thing for thee to have left the Lord thy God. *Jer. ii.*

2. Did you ever think about the word *to leave, to go away*. From the west of Ireland the ships sail to America. One day a ship stood near the sea-coast ready to set off with emigrants for America. It was time for the ship to set sail, but still it waited. Some one who was to sail in that ship had not yet come. In a few moments some persons were seen coming out of the country on their way to the ship. They were father, mother, brothers, and sisters. One of the sisters was going to leave her family and sail to America. They had come to the seaside, and it was time for them to part and say good-bye—farewell to their sister who was going to leave them. If you had seen how they cried and sobbed,

if you had heard their screams at this last parting, you would have said their hearts were breaking. And now the ship had set off, and their sister had left them, and still the screams, and howlings of the desolate brothers and sisters come over the waters to the ship, piercing through the sound of the waves of the sea. Poor sinner, when God, who was more to you than father, mother, brother, or sister, was leaving you in the moment of mortal sin, did you scream, did you howl? No, sinner; look back, and you will remember that in that first moment of terrible and frightful lonesomeness *without God,* not a sigh, not a breathing of sadness, came from your heart.

3. My dear child, if you could go down into hell, and listen but for one single moment to the cry—the shriek—the howling of a damned soul—not because it burns in the unquenchable fire—but because it knows there what it is to lose God, then there would be no need for you to read in this book about losing God.

4. "When," says Jesus Christ, "you shall see the abomination of desolation standing in the holy place." *Mat. xxiv.* O sinner, you have seen that abomination of desolation standing in the holy place. Think of the day, the hour, the moment of your mortal sin; for in that moment the abomination of desolation began in your soul, which had been once the holy place of God, the temple of the Holy Ghost. If the sun was plucked out of the skies, and all the world was left in darkness, the world would be desolate, but the abomination of desolation would not be there, but in your soul, for it has lost not the sun, but the Creator of the sun. A river was cut off from its fountain head. The people mourned because the bed of their river was dried up. They had no water to drink, and they were desolate and died of thirst. But it is not the loss of the water of the earth which brings the abomination of desolation, for that is to be found only in the soul which has committed a mortal sin and lost Almighty God, the fountain head of justice. Oh, the dry and withered and parched up soul! *Jer. ii.* "They have forsaken me, the fountain of living water." It would be a cruel sight to see the eyes plucked out from the head, and nothing left but two bleeding holes. The poor creature would feel desolate, in his blindness; but this would not be the abomination desolation and lonesomeness, no,

that is to be found only in the soul which has committed mortal sin and lost the eye of God's providence. Oh, the abomination of desolation in the soul, great and deep as God himself, because the soul has lost God himself! A little child has lost a pin, and it cries for the loss of its pin. True, a pin is but a trifle, but still it is a loss, and that child shows that it knows what is meant by a loss. But you, O dull, stupid, ignorant sinner, surely you know not what is meant by a loss; for you have lost not a pin, but Almighty God, and you cry not. A traveller was going along the road and he met a little child crying bitterly. What is the matter? he said to the poor little creature; why do you cry? The child's voice was choked with sobs, and it could not answer. At length the child lifted up its hand and pointed to the ground. The traveller looked, and behold, he saw lying on the ground a little bottle, worth about a penny, broken. This child had, by accident, let the bottle fall, and it broke into pieces. O sinner, that child will be your condemnation at the judgement seat of Jesus Christ. It will say, O Christ, I cried and sobbed for this loss of a miserable bottle, and that sinner committed a mortal sin, and lost you, and he never shed one tear for losing you. Weep, then, O sinner; "let your eyes run down with tears, because the Comforter, the relief of your soul, is gone." *Lam. i.*

5. THE LOSS OF GOD'S IMAGE AND LIKENESS.— *Let us make man in our image and likeness. Gen. i. 26*. There was a gentleman who had a most beautiful picture. This picture was the wonder of the world; it was above all price. People came from all parts of the world to see it. It happened one day that an evil minded man came also to see the famous picture. Being alone in the room, he took a knife out of his pocket, and maliciously cut the picture into a thousand pieces. Great was the anger of the owner of the picture. He would rather have lost his whole fortune than lose that picture. The destruction of the famous picture was soon known over the whole world; every newspaper in Europe gave an account of it. Every one said that the destruction of the picture was a most malicious, a most unpardonable action. They said that the man must be mad. The picture was but the work of the hand of man. You, O sinner, had in your soul a picture done by the hand of God; it was a picture of God himself, the image and likeness of God was in your soul.

The angels wondered to see in your soul a picture of God so perfect and beautiful. "You were the seal of resemblance, perfect in beauty." *Ezech. xxviii.* Then came the fatal day, the day of mortal sin, and you, like a madman, by your mortal sin, broke in pieces the image and likeness of God, in your soul, and it was seen there no more, but in place of it, the horrible image and likeness of the devil. Weep, then, O sinner, weep for your loss, "let tears run down, like a torrent, night and day." *Lam. ii. 18.*

6. LOSS OF GRACE.—*You are fallen from grace. Gal. v. 4.* O sinner, God once breathed into your soul the breath of life. His justifying grace made it bright as the sun, beautiful as an angel of God. "The fame of thy beauty went forth through heaven and earth." *Ezech. xvi.* Then came the mortal sin, and the devils stripped you of the garments of salvation. They robbed you of the armor of God, which made you able to resist in the evil day, and to stand in all things perfect; they took away from you the breastplate of justice and the helmet of salvation; *Eph. vi.* Oh, stupid sinner, you lose your old threadbare coat, made of a bit of cloth, the work of men's hands, and you are anxious and troubled and seek it everywhere. You have lost the grace of God, the garments of salvation, so precious and beautiful that even the angels could not make them, and you cared nothing about it. Poor sinner, God has done to you what he said, *Ezech. xvi. 17.*: "Behold, I will stretch out my hand and take away thy justification." Weep, then, now at least, O sinner. "Let tears run down, like a torrent, night and day." *Lam. ii.*

7. LOSS OF GOD'S LIGHT.—"*He shall drive him out of light into darkness." Job xviii. Ps. vi. :* "Light is risen to the just." This light of heaven shines in the heart of the children of God, that they may see the path which is to lead them to heaven through this dark and sinful world. When you became the child of God, he called you also out of darkness into his admirable light, *1 Pet. ii.*, and you rejoiced in that light. But suddenly this light was put out in your soul, it was extinguished by mortal sin. Then, in your soul, you were a man who walks on the earth at midnight, when there are neither moon, nor stars, but only thick darkness. He loses his way, and he stumbles and he falls into ditches and pits, and he bruises himself, and he has no hope until the light returns.

In the city of Rome, under the ground, there are narrow passages many miles in length. They are long and winding, and crossing one another in every direction. These passages under ground are called the catacombs. The early Christians in times of persecution concealed themselves in these places; and even now one often meets there with little chapels, where the Christians worshipped God in secret when the persecutors would not suffer them to do it openly. People, now-a-days, often go down and visit these places; but then it is necessary that they should have a guide with them who knows the way, otherwise they would be lost amidst so many passages, turning and winding and crossing one another. The guide also carries a light before them, because these places, being under ground are dark as midnight. One day some German students went into the catacombs with a guide and a light. They went in, but they never came out again. People were sent to seek them, but they could never be found. It is thought that by some accident their light went out—that in the darkness it was impossible to find their way out again—and so they died of hunger, or perhaps they fell into some deep pit and perished. Poor sinner, the light of God is gone out in your soul! Now you are going forward in the dark. *Lam. iii. 6.* : "He hath set me in dark places." Stop, then, O sinner, stop, I beseech you, for perhaps the very next step you take you will drop into the pit of hell. A man is reading by the light of a candle, suddenly that light is put out, and he is in the dark—he starts with surprise. Oh, sinner, in the moment of mortal sin, the light of God was suddenly put out in your soul, and you did not start with surprise, you took no notice of it.

Forget not, then, that you are sitting in darkness, and in the shadow of death; *Luc. i.* What death is that in whose shadow you are sitting? Is it the death which at the end of life will set your soul free from your body? No, it is not that death—it is another death—it is called the second death; *Apoc. xx.* This death is in hell, and it does not itself come out of hell; but it sends its shadow up to you, and you sit in the shadow of death, as if you sat under the shade of a tree or a house. Lift up your eyes, O sinner, and look at that shadow of death which rears itself up and hangs over you. Yes, there it is; it rises up by your side. Oh, what a dark shadow it is—what a gloomy shadow it is! see how fierce it looks—how it threatens you. Hasten, then, O sinner, rush away out of that shadow of death, and fly to God who is always ready to enlighten those who sit in darkness and the shadow of death; *Luke i.*

8. LOSS OF GOOD WORKS.—*Aggeus ii. 18 : I struck all the works of your hand with the mildew.* There have been many unfortunate people who have lost their all, lost all they had in the world by fire, or by shipwreck, or by robbery, or by failing in business, and other ways. Kings have lost their crowns and thrones, rich men have lost their estates, soldiers have lost a battle, children have lost their parents, and parents their children. There have been some who could not bear their loss. They fell into a deep melancholy, or they lost their senses and were shut up in a madhouse; nay, even some have killed themselves. O sinner, you are the great loser; to you only the great loss came. You were rich beyond measure. During all those years that you were a child of God, He kept an account of every one of your thoughts, words, and actions done for his sake; and for each of them there was a reward ready for you in heaven, such as no eye hath seen, nor ear hath heard; *2 Cor. ii.* Then came the mortal sin and God struck out of the Book of Life all the works of your hands. You had laid up for yourself treasures in heaven, crowns, and thrones, and kingdoms. But the hour of mortal sin came, and the thieves, and the devils, broke through and stole all your treasures.

A man works for his master; he keeps a book, and he always writes in the book how many days in the week, how many hours in the day, he works for his master. A year has passed, and he goes to his master and shows him the account of all the days and the hours he has worked for him, then he asks to be paid for all his work. The master answers, "For all the works you have done for me, I pay you nothing." Thus God does to the sinner. The sinner says to God: I have kept your commandments, I have fasted and prayed, and given alms, what reward shall I have? God answers: For all the prayers, and fasts, and good works you have done, I shall give you no reward at all. Why not, asks the sinner? Because, God answers, because you have committed a mortal sin, and the promise, the covenant I made to reward you, is made void. *Zach. xi. 11.*

"Thou fool;" *Luke xii.* A man breaks in pieces his chairs and tables; he sets his house on fire, and burns it down; he throws all his money into the river. The people cry out that he has lost his senses, he is mad. They come and seize hold of him, and bind him, and carry him away to the mad-house, and shut him up in the mad-house. Why do they say that he is mad? Because he wilfully destroyed his own property. You, O sinner! did you not wilfully commit that mortal sin, and did you not know that by mortal sin you cast away heaven and all its treasures? Then you are the madman and the fool, and your end will be shut up in hell, the great mad-house for the fools who wilfully throw away heaven and its treasures, bought for them with the precious blood of Jesus Christ.

Wisd. xv. 17 : "He formed a dead thing with his wicked hands." Your past good works then are lost. But, perhaps, you will make up your loss by your future good works. No, sinner, so long as you remain in mortal sin, an enemy of God, there will be no reward in heaven for any good works you may do. The covenant of God to reward you is made void; *Zach. xi.* Your hand is withered and can no more work for the works of God. Do you know what is meant by "a man being out of work?" He may work as he pleases, but he gets no pay for it. The factory has stopped, there are no more wages. Poor, sinner, you are out of the work of God, you can get no more wages in heaven. But although the good works you do in a state of mortal sin will not be rewarded in heaven, still it is good to do them, because they will, perhaps, move God to give you the peace of repentance, and then you will get back again your good works now lost. *Dan. iv.* : "Redeem thy sins with alms, and thy iniquities with works of mercy to the poor, and perhaps God will forgive thy offences."

9. LOSS OF VIRTUES.—*Luke i. 53* : *The rich he hath sent away empty.* You were rich in all virtues while you were yet a child of God. But where are these virtues now since mortal sin— where are they? A ship, filled with riches, was sailing over the ocean; the storms came, and the waves were dashed against the ship, and the winds blew it against the rocks, and it was broken in pieces. When the storm was over, the people came down to the sea-shore to see what there was of the ship. Behold, they could see only a few broken blanks floating on the water, the rest

was sunk to the bottom of the sea. So it was with your virtues, O sinner, when your soul was shipwrecked by mortal sin. See that child which has lately committed a mortal sin; you can tell it by its very look. *Is. ii.* : "The show of their face hath answered them." It has lost all the power and strength of virtue; it hangs down its head: it is ashamed of itself, like Adam and Eve were ashamed of themselves after their sin, and went to hide themselves behind the trees in Paradise. It no longer loves to be in chapel and at its prayers, for it feels that God has no respect for is offerings; *Gen. iv. 5*. It is no longer cheerful in obeying its parents; it has become quite selfish, for "he that is evil to himself, to whom will he be good?" *Eccus. xvi.*

10. THE LOSS OF ALL.—*The whole world shall fight with him against the sinner. Wisd. v.* O sinner! in those happy days before mortal sin, when God was with you, temptations and tribulations came upon you, but what harm could they do you? If God be for us, who is against us? *Rom. viii.* Yes, rather, by the most sweet providence of God all these things worked together for your good; *Rom. viii.* Poor sinner! look round the wide world, and you will see that you have not one friend. The sun sees you, and it hates to shine upon you, as it became dark, and would not shine on those who, like you, crucified Jesus Christ; *Mark xv.* I will make the lights of heaven to mourn over thee; *Ezech. xxxii.* Hearken! the winds sigh over you because you have become the enemy of Him, who breathed into your soul the breath of life. See the beasts of the earth and the birds of the air fly from you, because you are God's enemy; the earth hates to bear your footsteps, even as it trembled and shook under the feet of those who nailed Jesus to the cross; *Matt. xxvii.*

11. THE SORROWFUL ENDING.—Luke xv. : He went abroad into a far country; and there came a mighty famine in that country, and he began to be in want. And he would fain have filled his belly with the husks the swine did eat; and no man gave unto him. O sinners in mortal sin, listen to a sorrowful story. There was a certain wicked child, a little girl of about eight or nine years of age. She was very wicked; cursing and stealing, and going into all kinds of bad company. Often had her father spoken to her and told her not to offend God by her sins. She listened not to her father. One day he spoke thus to her, My little

child, he said, you are leading a very wicked life, and you not only do harm to yourself, but you give bad example to your brothers and sisters. I give you two weeks, and if at the end of two weeks you are not better, I must send you away out of the house, lest your brothers and sisters should learn to follow your bad example. The two weeks passed; the child was no better, but worse. One morning her father led her to the street door, and opening it, he said: My child, I told you that unless you became better I should be obliged to send you away; and now you are no better, so you may go away out of this house till you are willing to be good. The child answered not a word to its father, but proudly and sullenly it walked away. It wandered about the streets all the day, and got nothing to eat. In the evening when it began to be dark, the child was faint with hunger, and weary and tired with walking about. It knew not where to go and lay its head down and sleep. At last it found a heap of stones at the corner of some street, and it laid its sorrowful head there and slept. Next morning the child rose up from its stones and began to wander again about the streets. Great was its hunger; and it said to itself, Perhaps when the people see me look so pale and hungry, they will have pity on me, and give me something to eat. As it went along it sometimes looked up into the faces of those who passed it, thinking they would be moved with pity, but nobody took the least notice of the child. The second evening was come, and the poor child had eaten nothing all the day. It was too proud to go back home, and say, Father I am very sorry that I have been so bad; but if you will let me come and be with my brothers and sisters again, I will try to be good. Weak with hunger, the poor child was ready to fall down; and with difficulty it crept back again to its stones to sleep. During the night the wind blew hard and the rain fell in torrents, and every rag that the child had on was soaked with rain. It was midnight, and the child felt a burning fever. The dark hours passed over its burning head. Next morning, when the light dawned, the child was not able to stand on its feet; and before the sun rose, the poor creature had breathed out its last breath, and lay dead on the stones. Some one passing by that way saw the dead body of a child lying on the stones, and soon a crowd of people gathered round it. Having found out where the father lived, they carried the dead body of the child to his home. When the father saw the dead body of his poor little child carried into his house, oh, the grief, the sorrow of the father! his heart was broken when he saw his poor little child dead before his eyes. He never thought that such a thing would have happened; he thought when the child felt hungry it would have come back again to its home. The brothers and sisters came down stairs, and when they saw their poor little sister dead, they shriek! Then they came near, and leaned over their dead sister—their poor lost sister—and bitter tears fell down from their eyes, on the pale face of their dead sister. Then they said: Oh, poor sister! poor little sister, you are dead and we shall never see you again. When the people of the town heard what had happened, they came and stood round the windows and doors of the house, and they cried out against the father for the death of the child.

Little child in mortal sin, you who are reading this book, know that the very same thing which happened to that child has happened also to you. When you committed that mortal sin, you left a kind and good Father: your Father who is in heaven, Almighty God, the Father who created you. Oh, the grief, the sorrow of Jesus when he saw that your soul was dead; that soul which he loved so much, and for which he had died on the cross. The spirits of heaven who stood round him, saw that his sorrow in losing you was so great, that they thought his heart was breaking. What wonder that Jesus, who stood by the grave of Lazarus and cried for the death of his body, should be broken-hearted for the death of your soul? The angels in heaven cried bitter tears for a sister spirit that was dead. *Is. xxxiii. 7.* "Behold the angels of peace shall weep bitterly." But what happened in hell when your soul died by mortal sin? All hell was stirred up, shouts of blasphemy went up from hell to heaven on account of your mortal sin.

Poor soul! how art thou fallen, thou who didst arise from the waters of Baptism bright as an angel of God. Thou who wast the Throne of the Most High, now thou art trampled under foot by the devils! "God will send wrath and trouble to you by his evil angels." *Ps. lxxvii.* "He will lift up a sign to them, and, behold they will come with speed swiftly." *Is. v.*

CHAPTER VIII

THE DEVILS

1. "THE Spirit of the Lord departed from Saul, and an evil spirit troubled him." *1 Kings xvi.* You have an old shoe, good for nothing at all; the sides of it are bursting—the sole has fallen off. You do not want it any more. You throw it away. Then if anybody passes by that way and sees the old shoe, and picks it up, and wishes to have it, he has the right to have it, for it belongs to nobody, the owner threw it away. When the soul commits a mortal sin God hates it, and casts it away. *Ps. lxxxviii. 9* : "Thou hast rejected it." *Lam iii. :* "Thou hast made him an outcast." Then the devil, when he sees that God is casting away a soul, goes quickly to it and seizes it as a hungry dog would seize a bone. So, "'the Spirit of the Lord departed from Saul, and an evil spirit troubled him." *1 Kings xvi.* So, when Judas received the body and blood of Christ unworthily, then "Satan entered into him." *John xiii.*—It is not one devil only which comes into the soul, but many: "For their name was legion." *Luke viii.* Yes, O sinner, your soul "has fallen and is become the habitation of devils, and the hold of every unclean spirit." *Apoc. xiii.* "Demons and monsters shall meet there, and hairy ones shall cry out to one another." *Is. xxxiv.* Did you ever see a swarm of bees cluster round the branch of a tree? so the devils cluster round your soul, O sinner! *Ps. cxvii. 12 :* "They surrounded me like bees." They are in you as a brood of vipers; *Matt. viii.* When a dead body has been buried in the grave, the flesh is eaten up by worms; so a soul buried in the grave of mortal sin is devoured by the devils. *Job xxx. 17* : "They that feed upon thee do not sleep." You would see all this clearly, if God showed you the sight which he showed to the prophet Ezechiel. "Son of man," said God to the

prophet Ezechiel, "go in and see the wicked abominations. And I went in, and saw, and behold every form of creeping things and living creatures, the abominations." *Ezech. viii.* Would you be content to be thrown into a den full of lions, and tigers, and serpents, and adders, and asps, and scorpions, and toads, and spiders, and all kinds of venomous, stinging reptiles? Your soul itself, O sinner, is the den and the hole of the reptiles of hell. For your throat is an open sepulchre to them; *Rom iii.* There in your soul is that devil who goeth about like a roaring lion seeking whom he may devour; *Pet. v.* It is that same lion of which David said, "Save me, O Lord, lest he seize upon my soul like a lion, while there is none to save me." *Ps. vii.* You, O sinner, did not cry out to God to save you from mortal sin. Therefore, that lion has seized upon you and devours you; *Apoc. xii.* The great, frightful dragon is in your soul, crushing it like a millstone crushes that which it falls upon. *Lam. iii. :* "To crush under his feet all the prisoners of the land." That devil, exceeding fierce, is in your soul, who made you break in pieces the bonds and fetters of the law of God, and cast his yoke from you; *Ps. ii.* Those unclean spirits are in your soul, who, with great violence, carried two thousand swine headlong into the sea; *Mark v.* Poor soul, how swiftly they carry you. And wither do they carry you? To hell. There is in your soul that devil, who, while yet you walked in the ways of the Lord, seized you and threw you down into mortal sin; *Mark ix.* But see, what is that terrible form which winds and coils itself round and round your soul like ivy winds itself round a tree? O that terrible twisted creature! it is the form of a serpent. But what a serpent! We have heard of huge boa-constrictor serpents, which, from the trees of the forest, throw themselves upon wild beasts, upon elephants, and twisting themselves round and round those beasts, crush them to death. We have heard of rattle-snakes stinging people to death. But that serpent twisted round you, O sinner, is no boa-constrictor, no rattle-snake, it is not a serpent of the earth, but a serpent of hell! Oh, that terrible fierce serpent twined round your soul, how dark and slimy! how its twisted and poisonous folds rise and fall like the waves of the sea! Poor sinner, that serpent has gone round and round your whole soul, and round every faculty of it—will, memory, and understanding. You exist only within the folds of that serpent.

But see, the serpent has raised up its great, fierce, cruel head, and from its dark mouth it shoots out its forked and fiery tongue, hissing at you, biting at you. *Jer. viii. 17* : "Behold I will send among you serpents, basilisks, against which there is no charm, they shall bite you, saith the Lord." See how he breathes into you his poisoned, fiery breath. *Job. xli. 12* : "Flame cometh out of his mouth."

But see that sting, that sharp, subtle, penetrating, infernal diabolical sting. That sting is called "the sting of death." *1 Cor. xv.* It is not as the sting of the wasp, or the sting of a scorpion, for these stings can sting only the flesh; but that diabolic sting stings the soul. But, thanks be to God, this infernal sting cannot pierce those who have the sign of God; *Apoc. ix.* But from you, O sinner, the sign of the living God was taken away at the moment of mortal sin, and now that stinging serpent-demon ceases not to thrust his infernal sting into your soul. This serpent is that same subtle serpent which went into Paradise to tempt Eve. But there is another devil in your soul, whose feet are swift to shed blood; *Rom. iii.* He is the murderer of your soul, hacking and cutting it in pieces. It is that devil who was a murderer from the beginning; *John viii.* See how "in his wrath he strikes your soul with an incurable wound, and persecutes it in a cruel manner." *Is. xiv.* But listen! that is that sound—that word, that diabolical word spoken in your soul, O sinner? Surely that voice has been heard on the earth before. It sounds like the voice of him who once said, "No, you shall not die the death." Yes, it is the voice of the devil who is a liar and the father of lies; *John viii.* What does he say? He deals deceitfully with his tongue. *Ps. v.* He devours your soul, he crushes it in pieces, he stings it, he poisons it. Yet he says to you, "No, this cannot be true, because you feel nothing—you feel no teeth, no stings, no poison." But one thing, O sinner, you forget. You forget that the soul which is in you is a dead soul! Now, tell me, the dead body which is lying in the grave, does it feel the worms that are eating it? The sheep, which has been slain, does it feel the sharp knife of the butcher which cuts it in pieces. The beast which lies dead on the field, does it feel the beaks of the wild birds which tear its flesh away from its bones? Yes, it is quite true that you do not feel these things, and that word "you do not feel" should break your heart, because it reminds you that your soul lives no more, that it is a dead thing cast away.

2. Oh, sinner, there is nobody on the earth who accuses you. There is nobody who cries out that you have committed a mortal sin. It seems as if heaven and earth were silent and your sin forgotten. But there is one who accuses you night and day before God. *Apoc. xii.* Your accuser is the devil. Would you know how the devil accuses you? There was a certain person who committed a mortal sin. God let one of his saints see what the devil did at that moment. The earth opened by the side of the sinner, and a black devil rose up out of hell. He was one of those devils "who are kept under darkness in everlasting chains unto the judgement of the great day." *Jude 6.* This devil held in his hand, a fiery chain, which he put round and round the dead soul of the sinner, till the whole soul, and every faculty of it, was fast bound with this fiery chain. "They shall keep fast hold of their prey." *Is. v.* Therefore this devil kept hold of fiery chain, and followed the sinner withersoever he went, although the sinner himself saw nothing and knew it not. He was one of those demons of whom it is said, "He goeth about." *1 Pet. v.* If the man walked along the road, this noonday devil, *Ps. xc.,* followed him, holding him by the chain. In his workshop the devil held him by the chain; at his meals the devil was by his side, holding him by the chain; even in the chapel of the devil, who can transform himself into an angel of light, *2 Cor. xi.,* held the man by the infernal chain. *2 Pet. ii. 4.* In the night time the devil, "who walketh about in the dark," *Ps. xc.* stood at his bedside, holding him fettered with the bonds of darkness. *Wisd. xvii.* It seemed as if from time to time the devil lifted up his face to heaven and said some prayer to God. What could it be? how could the devil pray? *Job i.* That Satan, who on a certain day when the sons of God came to stand before the Lord, was also present among them to pray for evil on Job, prayed thus. "O God!" the devil said, "you sentence to the eternal flames of hell those who commit a mortal sin, and thou art a just God, and thy judgements are true and just. O God, that sinner whom thou hast commanded me to bind with the chains of hell has committed a mortal sin, he has not repented, and now he sleeps with that mortal sin in his soul. May this sleep be his last sleep! O God, let thy sentence against this sinner now be

executed. Bid me to strike him and kill him, now while he sleeps, and carry his soul down to hell." Poor sinner, the devil is also at this moment at your side, holding you fast bound with his fiery chain, and praying to God night and day that he may carry you to hell. Thus does the devil bind in the chains of hell those who commit a mortal sin, in that bond with which all sinners are tied. *Is. xxv.;* even as that woman whom Satan had bound for eighteen years, so that she was bent double and could not look upwards. *Luke xiii.*

Thus, poor sinner, the Lord hath done that which he proposed; he hath fulfilled the word which he commanded in the days of old. *Gen. ii.* "He hath destroyed and hath not spared, he hath caused the enemy to rejoice over thee." *Lam ii. 7.*

CHAPTER IX

MORTAL SIN WRITTEN IN CHARACTERS OF FIRE

WHEN you committed that mortal sin, hell below was stirred up, and was in an uproar. *Is. xiv.* The black Book of Death, with the names of the damned written on its pages was opened; the crash of that terrible book when it was opened was as the sound of thunder. The wicked spirits in hell knew well the meaning of that sound. They knew that some poor creature on the earth had been committing a mortal sin, and that the name of that sinner was about to be written in the Book of Death. Then might be seen millions on millions of wicked spirits with spiteful joy gathering round the terrible book to see whose name it was. Then came the writing in letters of fire; your name, the sin you committed, the day, the hour, the moment of it, the place, the manner. After this came the terrible sentence, that you were from that moment a "child of hell." There was the sentence; and now, O sinner, you only wait the execution of that sentence.

Poor sinner, there is still One who has pity on you, and is sorrowful for you, and he wishes to speak to you. Listen to him.

CHAPTER X

THE VOICE OF GOD TO THE SINNER

※

POOR sinner! God says to you: I loved you with an everlasting love. *Jer. xxxi.* I created you, and breathed into your soul the breath of life, and made you to be my child, beautiful as an angel of heaven. Then I could not bear to be absent from you, so I came myself to dwell in your soul, that I might always be with you, and love you, and take care of you. But, behold, there came to me a sorrowful moment; you cast me away from you, you would not have me for your Father any more. Poor sinner! why did you leave me? what was it for? what harm did I ever do to you? I created in your soul a light which should never fail, but you loved to have darkness rather than the light. *John iii.* I gave you life everlasting that you might live forever, *John vi.,* but you chose to have death rather than life. I gave you peace and joy of heart, *Gal. v.* and you have chosen rather to have the thorn of anguish fastened in your heart. *Ps. xxxi.* I gave you the bread of life, and you have brought to me the poison of death—mortal sin. I so loved you that I gave you my beloved Son, Jesus, and with him I gave you all things, and behold you have treated my sweet Son, Jesus, disgracefully, crucifying him again, trampling under foot his most precious blood, and choosing rather to have the devil for your master. *Heb. vi.*

O soul! created to my image and likeness, and redeemed by the blood of my Son, Jesus, and sanctified by my Holy Spirit, in what did I offend you that you should do thus to me? Poor soul, remembering the days of old when you were my child, and grieving to see that you are on the road to hell, I come to you now to ask you to return to me; it is not too late—still there is time, but if you delay longer, perhaps it will be too late. Come back, then, to me, and be my child as you were before, for, as I live, I will not the death of a sinner, but that he be converted and lives. *Ezech. xxxiii.*

CHAPTER XI

MORTAL SIN WRITTEN IN CHARACTERS OF BLOOD

※

"BALAAM of Bosor had a check of his madness, the dumb beast used to the yoke." *2 Pet. ii.* St. Ambrose tells a story about a little dog. The dog was a beautiful creature. It loved its master; it would lick his hand and eat out of it, and follow him where ever he went. It was a faithful dog. In the night time if robbers came to the door, the dog would bark at them; when the robbers heard the dog barking they would say, We had better go away, for the dog is barking, and we shall be found out. One day the master of the dog went out of the house. When he came back his face was covered—he had a mask on. He opened the door and walked in. The dog did not know him again because his face was covered. So it barked at him, jumped on him, and bit slightly the end of his finger, which began to bleed. Then the master uncovered his face, and the dog, looking up, saw that it had been biting its own master. Great was the sorrow of the little dog when it found that it had been biting its own master. It lay down on the floor with its head on the ground, and began to moan most sorrowfully. Then the master came to it, and patting it on the head, said, Never mind, my poor little dog, you did not mean to bite me; look up at me. But the poor dog did not look up, and it never looked up in its master's face again. The master did every thing he could to take away the distress of the poor dog; he brought it bones to eat, and water to drink; but no—the poor dog would no more eat or drink. After a while the dog rose up and went down the steps which led to the cellar. When it came into the cellar it threw itself down into a deep hole. For three days and three nights the dog stopped in this hole, neither eating or drinking, but moaning most pitifully. Towards the end of the three days the moans became fainter and fainter, and at last its sorrowful moans were heard no more; the poor creature was dead. And this dog died of a broken heart—broken with sorrow, because it had accidentally, without meaning it, done a little injury to its master.

O sinner, learn a lesson from the dumb creature. Look up at the cross. On the cross there hangs Jesus Christ, your Master. Come near then, O sinner, come near to the cross, and look up at the face of Jesus Christ your Master. Can you look up at his face and say that you never did him any injury? What? you never did any injury to Jesus Christ! See those sharp thorns which pierce his dying head! See those sharp nails which fasten his wounded hands and feet to the cross! See that blood which runs down, not drop by drop, but in streams from the cross! See, Jesus bows down his head, and he breathes out his last breath—he is dead! Who is it that did all these injuries to Jesus Christ? O sinner, it is you who did all these cruel injuries to Jesus. Your mortal sin bruised his poor body and made him bleed. Your mortal sin was the hammer which nailed him to the cross "Crucifying again to yourself the Son of God." *Heb. vi.* Your mortal sin was the great heavy weight which wedged on the dying heart of Jesus, and broke it, and made him die of sorrow. Yes, he was wounded for your iniquities, and bruised for your sins; *Is. liii.* O sinner, look up again at the face of the dying Jesus! Perhaps you are afraid to look at him. You think that Jesus is angry at you for the injuries you have done him. O sinner, you know not the sweet Jesus. No; he cannot look angry. See, poor sinner, he wants you to look at him, he wants you to see that his last look before he dies is a look of mercy, of compassion, of love for your poor soul. Hearken, poor sinner, Jesus speaks to you.

CHAPTER XII

THE VOICE OF JESUS ON THE CROSS TO THE SINNER

※

"POOR sinner," Jesus says, "you went away from me by mortal sin, and now I want you to come back to me and be again my child. When on the cross I cried out that word, 'I thirst,' *John xix.*, I was thirsting for the moment to come when you would return to me. O sinner, why will you not come to me again? why may I not love you again? See, my arms are stretched out to receive you—my head is bowed down to give you the kiss of peace and forgiveness. The blood runs down from my body to wash away your sins. My heart is breaking with sorrow because you have left me. Come then to me, my dear sinner, I will make your repentance very easy—I will suffer for you the punishment due to your sins. Come, then, poor sinner, come and dwell under the shadow of my cross, and be again as you were before, my child and my brother. I will love you again, and you will give glory to my Father in heaven, and joy to his holy angels."

O Jesus, you have spoken sweet and gracious words of love and forgiveness; listen then to the poor sinner, for he is kneeling at the foot of the cross, and he wants to speak to you.

CHAPTER XIII

THE VOICE OF THE SINNER TO JESUS

※

O JESUS, my God, my Creator, what you say is most true. I remember how you were nailed to the hard cross—how your poor head was torn with the sharp thorns—how the holy blood came from your blessed body. Sweet Jesus, your blessed heart has spoken to me, and told me that you died a bitter death on the cross, for the love of me, your poor child, to wash away my sins with your precious blood, and to save me from hell. Yes, it was my sins which nailed you to the cross and made you die. Oh, wicked sins, I hate and detest you. My good Jesus, I love you, and I am very sorry for offending you, and I promise you that I will never offend you any more—no, never again. May I live for you and for you only, my sweet Saviour Jesus, and if you foresee that on any day of my future life I shall again offend you by mortal sin, may I not live to see that sorrowful day; in your sweet mercy take me out of this world before that day comes. Jesus, have pity on my poor soul! You did not turn away your face from those who struck it and spit upon it, will you turn away your face from a soul which wants to love you? O Jesus, think how much it cost you to save my soul. You bought it with your own blood—yes, you died for it; and now, my Jesus, I do not ask you to die again for me; I only ask you to say to me the one word—pardon, forgiveness. Do not refuse to save a soul which you died to save.

CHAPTER XIV

THE FUTURE

※

I. How to keep out of mortal sin.

1. *Keep away from what is likely to lead you into mortal sin.* Keep away from bad company; keep away from those companions who have already led you into sin; keep away from those places where you know there is danger of mortal sin; keep away from those bad books which have done you so much harm. If you ask me why you must keep away from these dangers, my answer is the word of God: "He that loveth the danger, shall perish in it." *Eccus. iii.*

2. *In time of temptation pray.* Jesus Christ says, "Watch ye, and pray, that ye enter not into temptation." *Matt. xxvi. 41.* The reason why people commonly fall into mortal sins is, because when temptation comes, they neglect to pray, and then God does not help them, and so they fall. Therefore, when temptation shall come, whether it be some wicked thought in your heart from the devil, or evil words, or bad example, always be ready to say the beautiful prayer of St. Alphonsus: "Jesus and Mary, help me." Every day pray that God would never let you commit a mortal sin, saying that petition of the Our Father, "Lead us not into temptation." You may also pray thus: "My God, with your help I resolve never to commit a mortal sin; may I die rather than commit a mortal sin."

3. If you wish to keep out of mortal sin, go often to the Sacraments, at least once a month. St. Alphonsus says, that the best way to keep out of mortal sin is to go to confession and the Holy Communion once every week. *John vi.* : "He that eateth this bread shall live forever."

4. Carefully avoid willful venial sins, and then be sure that you will avoid mortal sins. *Eccus. xix.* : "He that despiseth small things, shall fall by little and little."

5. Therefore, remember three things. 1. Keep away from the temptation. 2. In time of temptation say: "Jesus and Mary, help me." 3. Go often to the Sacraments.

II. What you must do if you have the misfortune to fall into mortal sin.

Jer. viii. : "Shall not he that falleth rise again?" If you catch a fever, you get rid of it as soon as you can. If you break your arm, you get it mended as soon as you are able. Do at least as much for your soul as for your body. If you commit a mortal sin, and you die with that mortal sin in your soul, you go to hell for all eternity! Therefore, do not keep that horrible monster, mortal sin, in your soul for one moment. But you say, "What must I do? which is the way? how am I to get this sin forgiven?" Listen and you shall hear what you must do: *Make an act of contrition directly, and go to confession as soon as you can.* Remember these two things.

1. *After mortal sin make an act of contrition directly.* Do not delay for a day, an hour, a minute, a moment. Say any act of contrition; for example, the act of contrition of blessed Leonard: "O my God, I am very sorry that I have sinned against thee, because thou art so good, and I will not sin again." But you say, What is the use of making an act of contrition directly after a mortal sin? I know I can get my sin forgiven by going to confession, but what is the use of making an act of contrition until the time comes when I can go to confession. I will tell you the use of it. It may be some days, it may be a week, before you can get to confession. Do you think God wishes you to remain in mortal sin for a week, or until the time comes when you can go to confession? Certainly he does not. But you can get your sins forgiven before you go to confession? Certainly, you can. But how? Through the great mercy of God, at any moment of the day or night, whenever you will, if you make a sincere act of true contrition, with the intention of confessing it, at that moment God forgives the sin, and you become the child of God again. How good God is, that a sinner should not be obliged to remain in mortal sin, and a state of damnation, one moment longer than he wishes it himself! St. Thomas says: "However little the sorrow

may be, if it is only true contrition, it takes away the sin." Q. 1, 2, 4. But you ask, what does St. Thomas mean when he says, "that this sorrow must be true contrition?" He means just this, that you must be sorry for offending God *because he is so good*, and resolve not to offend him again. St. Alphonsus says just the same; *Die Poenit. iv.*

In the lives of the Fathers of the Desert, we read of a holy man called St. Paul the Simple. He stood one Sunday at the church door while the people were going in to hear Mass. God let him see the state of their souls. Their angel guardians went along with them, showing great joy and contentment. But amongst them he saw one over whose head there was a dark cloud. His soul was black. The devil held him by a chain. His angel guardian followed at a distance, looking very sorrowful, with his eyes cast down on the ground. This man was in mortal sin. When the people came out again, St. Paul watched for the unfortunate man who was in mortal sin. At length he saw him; and, behold, the dark cloud which was over him had passed away—the chain no longer bound him, and his soul was shining with brightness. The devil stood at a great distance from him; his angel guardian was at his side rejoicing. St. Paul then went up to the man, and asked him what had happened to him while he was at Mass. The man answered: When I went into the church, I was in mortal sin. While I was in the church I happened to hear some words from the prophet Isaias, in which God promises to pardon those who repent sincerely. Then I began to pray. I said: O my God, you came into the world to save sinners; save me, for I am a great sinner, and most unworthy of your pardon. I am very sorry that I have sinned against you, because you are so good, and I promise you, with a sincere heart, that, from this moment, I will not sin any more. I will serve you for the time to come with a sincere conscience. Pardon a sinner who begs of you to forgive his sins. When St. Paul heard this, he cried out: Oh, the unspeakable goodness of God; how great is his compassion and love for poor sinners? Learn, then, O sinner, that the good and merciful God is ever ready to forgive your sin, at any moment and in any place, if you only make a good and sincere act of contrition. Learn, also the blessing of going to Mass on Sundays. How can a sinner pray with a sincere heart before the Divine blood on the altar, which washes away the sins of the world, and not have his sins forgiven?

3. Besides making an act of contrition directly after mortal sin, you should also go to confession, and *confess the sin as soon as you can*. First, because you are obliged to confess every mortal sin. Jesus Christ has instituted the sacrament of Penance, to forgive all mortal sins to those who are contrite of heart, and confess them sincerely. *John xx.* : "Whose sins you shall forgive, they are forgiven them." Secondly, although you may hope that the mortal sin has been forgiven, if you made a sincere act of contrition, still you feel more secure about the forgiveness of it, after you have received absolution in the sacrament of Penance.

There is one great evil, and only one.

The one great evil is—mortal sin.

From mortal sin, sweet Jesus, deliver us.

CATHOLIC WAY PUBLISHING
PAPERBACKS AND E-BOOKS

※

True Devotion to Mary: With Preparation for Total Consecration
by Saint Louis De Montfort
    5" x 8" Paperback: .ISBN–13: 978-1-78379-000-5
    6" x 9" Hardback: ISBN–13: 978-1-78379-004-3
    Kindle E-Book: ISBN–13: 978-1-78379-001-2
    EPUB E-Book: ISBN–13: 978-1-78379-002-9

The Secret of the Rosary by Saint Louis de Montfort
    5" x 8" Paperback: .ISBN–13: 978-1-78379-310-5
    Kindle E-Book: ISBN–13: 978-1-78379-311-2
    EPUB E-Book: ISBN–13: 978-1-78379-312-9

The Mystical City of God by Venerable Mary of Agreda
Popular Abridgement
    5" x 8" Paperback: .ISBN–13: 978-1-78379-063-0
    Kindle E-Book: ISBN–13: 978-1-78379-064-7
    EPUB E-Book: ISBN–13: 978-1-78379-065-4

The Imitation of Christ by Thomas a Kempis
    5" x 8" Paperback: .ISBN–13: 978-1-78379-037-1
    Kindle E-Book: ISBN–13: 978-1-78379-038-8
    EPUB E-Book: ISBN–13: 978-1-78379-039-5

My Daily Prayers by Catholic Way Publishing
    5" x 8" Paperback: .ISBN–13: 978-1-78379-027-2
    Kindle E-Book: ISBN–13: 978-1-78379-028-9
    EPUB E-Book: ISBN–13: 978-1-78379-029-6

The Three Ages of the Interior Life: Prelude of Eternal Life
by Reverend Reginald Garrigou-Lagrange O.P.
Volume One
    5" x 8" Paperback: .ISBN–13: 978-1-78379-296-2
    Kindle E-Book: ISBN–13: 978-1-78379-297-9
    EPUB E-Book: ISBN–13: 978-1-78379-298-6

Volume Two
    5" x 8" Paperback: .ISBN–13: 978-1-78379-299-3
    Kindle E-Book: ISBN–13: 978-1-78379-300-6
    EPUB E-Book: ISBN–13: 978-1-78379-301-3

CATHOLIC WAY PUBLISHING

WWW.CATHOLICWAYPUBLISHING.COM
LONDON, UK
2013

Made in the USA
Charleston, SC
09 March 2014